EVERYBODY'S FAVORITE SERIES 101

SELECTED FLUTE SOLOS

This classic collection provides the student and teacher a unique sourcebook of compositions chosen for their technique, phrasing, and melodic beauty. Includes the piano accompaniment.

FLUTE PART

GW00656031

AMSCO PUBLICATIONS
NEW YORK/LONDON/SYDNEY

VAR 060
1295

Order No. AM 40403
US International Standard Book Number: 0.8256.2101.1

Exclusive Distributors:
Music Sales Corporation
257 Park Avenue South, New York, NY 10010
Music Sales Limited
8/9 Frith Street, London W1V 5TZ England
Music Sales Pty. Limited
120 Rothschild Street, Rosebery, Sydney NSW 2018, Australia

Printed in the United States of America by
Vicks Lithograph and Printing Corporation

SELECTED FLUTE SOLOS

Gavotte

FLUTE

Johann Sebastian Bach

Fantasie

FLUTE

Gabriel Fauré, Op. 79

Sonata No. 2

FLUTE

Georg Friedrich Handel

Andalouse

FLUTE

Emile Pessard, Op. 20

Legende Pastorale

from 'Scotch Scenes'

Benjamin Godard. Op. 138

FLUTE

Andante quasi adagio

Serenade

FLUTE

Georges Hüe

Fantasie Pastorale Hongroise

FLUTE

Albert Franz Doppler, Op. 26

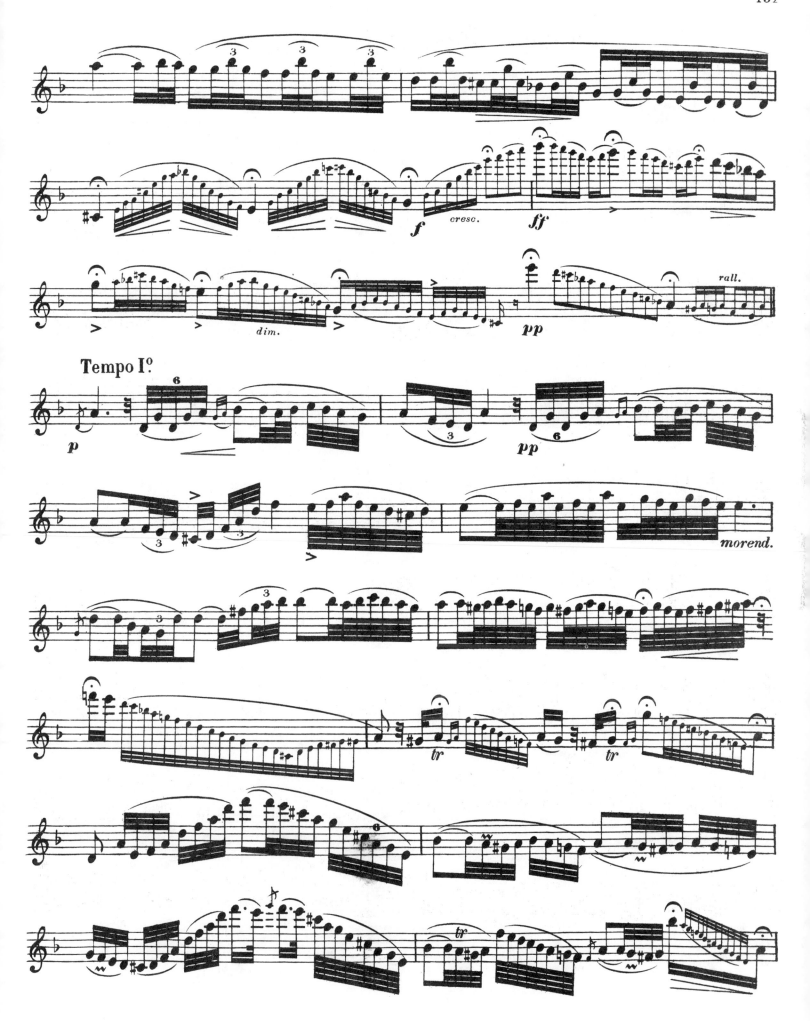

132

Melodie

from 'Orpheus'

Christoph W. von Gluck

FLUTE

Concertino

FLUTE

*Morceau de Concours
du Conservatoire National de Musique de Paris*

Cecile Chaminade, Op. 107

Poco rit.

a Tempo

J

K

Rit molto.

cadence.

rall.

rall.

ten.

ten.

ten.

L Tempo 1º

(1) Les 13 mesures comprises entre les signes ✳ ✳
ne se jouent pas avec l'accompagnement d'orchestre.

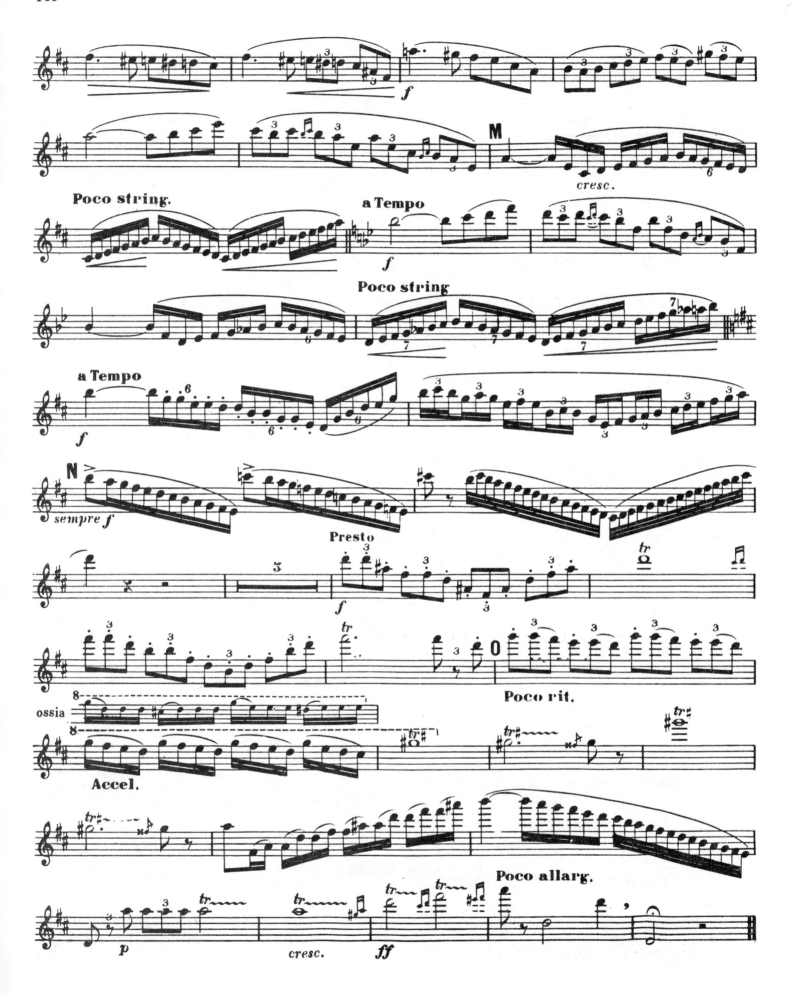

Scherzo

from 'A Midsummernight's Dream'

FLUTE

Felix Mendelssohn

Bolero

FLUTE

Emile Pessard, Op. 28, No. 2

Cadenzas

for Flute Concerto No. 2 K314
by W. A. Mozart

Joachim Andersen

FLUTE

Movement II

Movement III

Concerto No. 2

Wolfgang Amadeus Mozart, K314

FLUTE

154

159

EVERYBODY'S FAVORITE SERIES 101

SELECTED FLUTE SOLOS

*This classic collection provides the student and teacher a unique sourcebook of
compositions chosen for their technique, phrasing, and melodic beauty.
Includes the piano accompaniment.*

AMSCO PUBLICATIONS
NEW YORK/LONDON/SYDNEY

Order No. AM 40403
US International Standard Book Number: 0.8256.2101.1

Exclusive Distributors:
Music Sales Corporation
257 Park Avenue South, New York, NY 10010
Music Sales Limited
8/9 Frith Street, London W1V 5TZ England
Music Sales Pty. Limited
120 Rothschild Street, Rosebery, Sydney NSW 2018, Australia

Printed in the United States of America by
Vicks Lithograph and Printing Corporation

SELECTED FLUTE SOLOS

Gavotte

Johann Sebastian Bach

Allegro moderato

Trio

Scherzando

Fantasie

Gabriel Fauré, Op. 79

8

Sonata No. 2

Georg Friedrich Handel

Andalouse

Emile Pessard, Op. 20

Più moto

Légende Pastorale

(From "Scotch Scenes")

Benjamin Godard, Op. 138

Andante quasi adagio

Serenade

Georges Hüe

Fantasie Pastorale Hongroise

Albert Franz Doppler, Op. 26

48

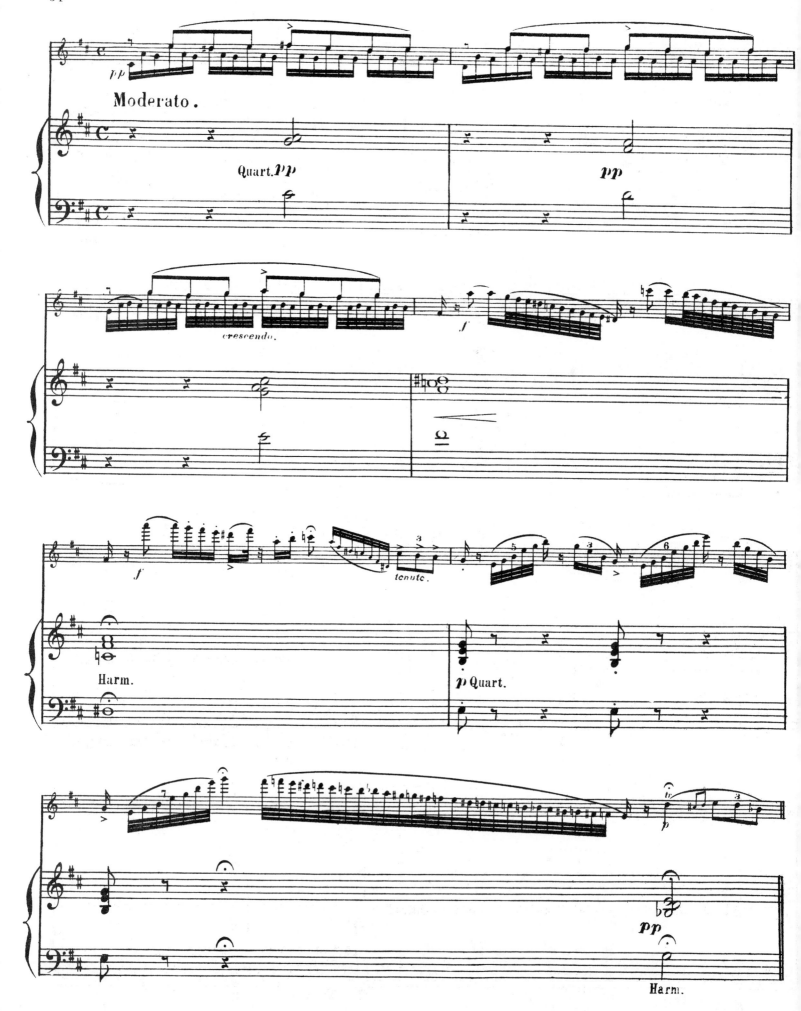

Melodie
from 'Orpheus'

Christoph W. von Gluck

Concertino

Morceau de Concours
du Conservatoire National de Musique de Paris

Cecile Chaminade, Op. 107

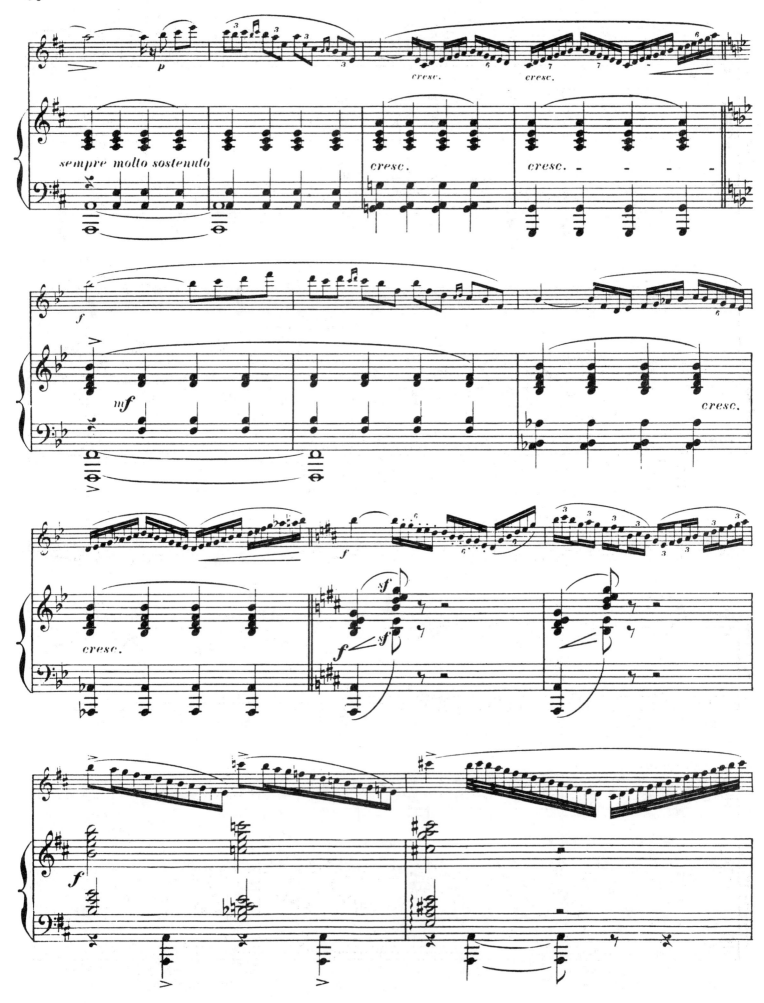

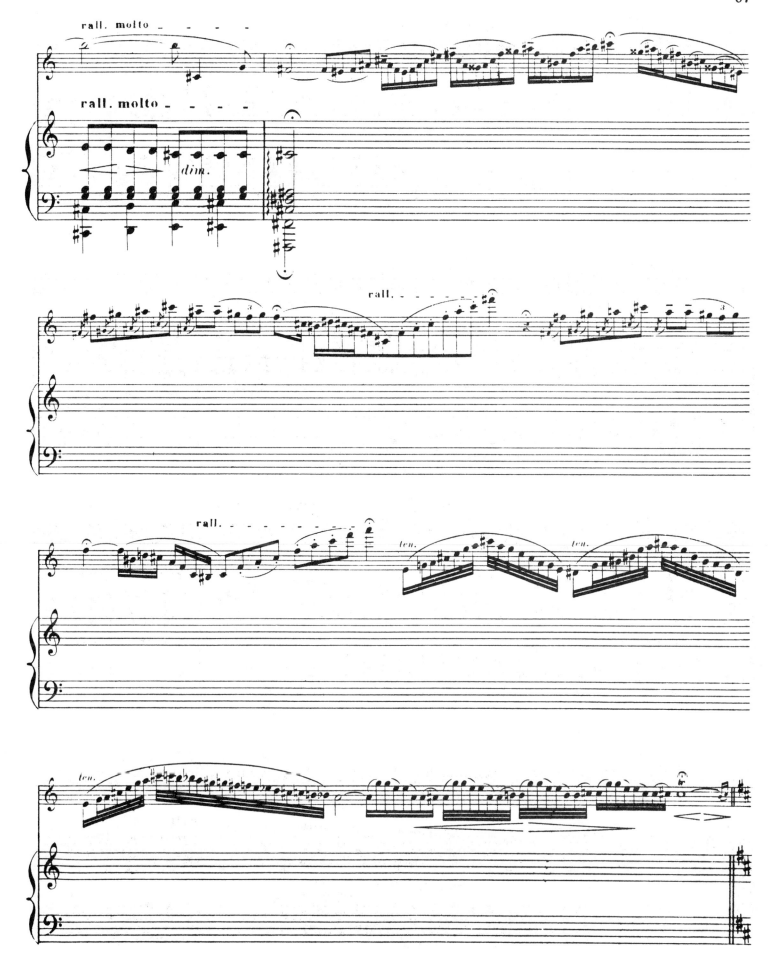

Scherzo
from 'A Midsummernight's Dream'

Felix Mendelssohn

Bolero

Emile Pessard, Op. 28, No. 2

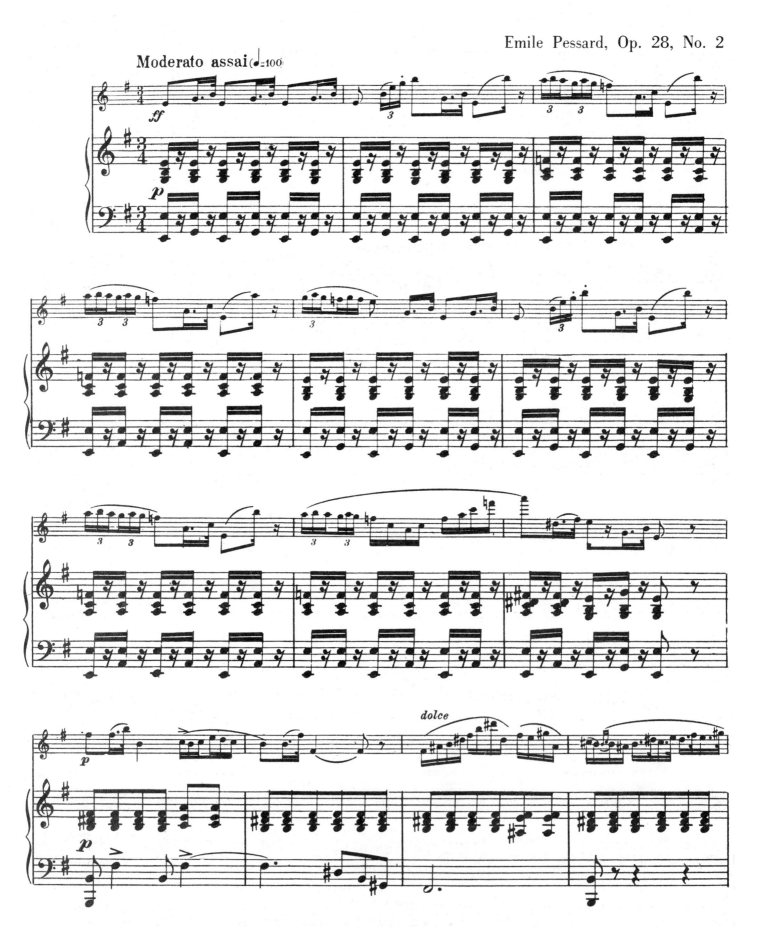

Pressez un peu

Concerto No. 2

Wolfgang Amadeus Mozart, K314

Allegro aperto.

Andante ma non troppo.